NETWORK MAILER 7

NETWORK MAILERS' MULTITUDE OF GIVERS

EARN $5,000,000.

LET THIS NETWORK MAILER SHOW YOU HOW TO DO IT.

Larry Smith Crockett

COPYRIGHT 2006, 2015 NETWORK MAILER:

AUTHOR: LARRY SMITH CROCKETT

www.trafford.com

North America & international
toll-free: 1 888 232 4444 (USA & Canada)
fax: 812 355 4082

INTRODUCTION

EVERYONE WORKING THIS FINANCIAL PROSPECT IS COUNTED A NETWORK MAILER.
NETWORK MAILERS REPLYING TO NETWORK MAILERS INCREASES THE RATE OF REPLY AND THE FINANCIAL POTENTIAL.

FOLLOWING THE INSTRUCTIONS AS OUTLINED IN THIS BOOKLET WILL RESULT IN SOME SIGNIFICANT WORKING CASH.

THE WORK OF THIS FINANCIAL PROSPECT IS A MAIL ORDER BUSINESS.

THIS BUSINESS REQUIRES PATIENT CONTINUANCE IN MAILING THE ENCLOSED CIRCULAR (THE NETWORK MAILER'S GIFT BUSINESS) TO A MAILING LIST.

AN ADDRESS OF A COMPANY WHERE YOU CAN RECEIVE A FREE COPY OF THEIR ADVERTISING MAGAZINE 'SHORE TO SHORE' IS, AS FOLLOWS:
CHA SERVICE
P.O. BOX 1980
ROGUE, OR 97537 USA
THIS MAGAZINE SERVES AS A SOURCE OF REPLY PROSPECTS.
$5,000,000 MAKES THIS FINANCIAL PROSPECT WORTH WORKING.

THE WORKING OF THIS FINANCIAL PROSPECT IS SMALL COMPARED TO THE FINANCIAL GAIN IT COULD RESULT IN.

THIS MARKET IS VERY HUGE; FOR EXAMPLE, IT WOULD TAKE 500 YEARS TO MAIL TO 150,000,000 DIFFERENT MAILING ADDRESSES MAILING 300,000 CIRCULARS PER YEAR.

HELP WHERE NEEDED MOST IS A BETTER MOTIVATION.

ENCLOSED IS A DIAGRAM OF AN ANALOGICAL MAILING CIRCUIT, AFTER YOUR BUSINESS IS ESTABLISHED WHERE NETWORK MAILERS ARE REPLYING TO NETWORK MAILERS.

2°B'S   →3°C'S
↑

20 DAYS

1°A←   4°D'S ↓

FINANCIAL POTENTIAL

THE FINANCIAL POTENTIAL IS PRINTED ON THE ENCLOSED MAILING CIRCULAR (THE NETWORK MAILER'S GIFT BUSINESS).
$5,000,000 MAKES THIS FINANCIAL PROSPECT WORTH WORKING.

THIS FINANCIAL PROSPECT DOES NOT INVOLVE MAILING AN ILLEGAL CHAIN LETTER.
THIS MAIL ORDER BUSINESS IS A GIFT GIVING FINANCIAL PROSPECT.

LET YOUR GOAL BE TO CONTINUE UNTIL A GROUP OF NETWORK MAILERS REPLYING TO NETWORK MAILERS IS FORMED.
LET REPLYING NETWORK MAILERS REPLYING TO NETWORK MAILERS BE YOUR MAILING LIST. WHERE YOU HAVE A GROUP OF NETWORK MAILERS HAVING THE SAME MAILING LIST AND REPLYING TO ONE ANOTHER, THE RATE OF REPLY IS GREATER AS WELL AS THE FINANCIAL POTENTIAL.

NETWORK MAILERS WORKING THIS FINANCIAL PROSPECT IS YOUR TOP PRIORITY MAILING LIST.

THE REPLIERS WILL BE TOO NUMEROUS TO INDEX.

USE LARGE PAPER BAGS TO KEEP THE REPLIERS ADDRESSES IN.
CODE THE BAGS TO KEEP RECORD OF YOUR MAILINGS.

REPEAT YOUR MAILINGS TO NETWORK MAILERS WORKING THIS FINANCIAL PROSPECT.

NETWORK MAILERS REPLYING TO NETWORK MAILERS INCREASES THE RATE OF REPLY AND THE FINANCIAL POTENTIAL.

IT TAKES ABOUT TWENTY MAILING DAYS FOR A MAILING CIRCUIT TO RUN ITS COURSE.

THIS IS AFTER YOU ESTABLISH THIS BUSINESS WHEN YOU HAVE A MAILING LIST OF REPEAT NETWORK MAILERS WORKING THIS FINANCIAL PROSPECT.

THE TIME FACTOR IS NOT AS LONG AS YOU MIGHT THINK TO ESTABLISH THIS BUSINESS.

$5,000,000 IS A FINANCIAL PROSPECT A LOT OF INDIVIDUALS WOULD WANT TO ENTER INTO THIS GIFTING PROGRAM WHERE IT WOULD ONLY COST AN OCCASIONAL FIVE U.S.A. DOLLARS.

AS I STATED PREVIOUSLY, THE WORKING OF THIS FINANCIAL PROSPECT IS SMALL COMPARED TO THE HUGE GAIN WHICH WILL RESULT IN WORKING IT.

THE HUGE MARKET IS WHAT MAKES THIS FINANCIAL PROSPECT WORK.

AS I STATED PREVIOUSLY, IT WOULD TAKE 500 YEARS TO MAIL TO 150,000,000 DIFFERENT MAILING ADDRESSES MAILING 300,000 PER YEAR.

SO, BY THIS, YOU CAN SEE THAT THE MARKET IS VERY HUGE.

THE WORKING OF THIS FINANCIAL PROSPECT IS DEPENDENT UPON A MULTITUDE OF NETWORK MAILERS COMMITTED TO FOLLOWING THE INSTRUCTIONS OF THE MAILING CIRCULAR ENCLOSED IN THIS BOOKLET.

THIS MAIL ORDER BUSINESS REQUIRES PATIENCE OF EVERY NETWORK MAILER WORKING THIS BUSINESS.

YOU HAVE TO KEEP RECORD OF THE REPLIERS.

REPEAT MAILING THE CIRCULAR TO THESE REPLIERS.

CHAIN LETTERS

FOLLOWING IS AN EXCERPT FROM THE UNITED STATES POSTAL INSPECTION SERVICE "CHAIN LETTERS".

"THERE'S AT LEAST ONE PROBLEM WITH CHAIN LETTERS. THEY'RE ILLEGAL IF THEY REQUEST MONEY OR OTHER ITEMS OF VALUE AND PROMISE A SUBSTANTIAL RETURN TO THE PARTICIPANTS. CHAIN LETTERS ARE A FORM OF GAMBLING, AND SENDING THEM THROUGH THE MAIL (OR DELIVERING THEM IN PERSON OR BY COMPUTER, BUT MAILING MONEY TO PARTICIPATE) VIOLATES TITLE 18, UNITED STATES CODE, SECTION 1302, THE POSTAL LOTTERY STATUTE. (CHAIN LETTERS THAT ASK FOR ITEMS OF MINOR VALUE, LIKE PICTURE POSTCARDS OR RECIPES, MAY BE MAILED, SINCE SUCH ITEMS ARE NOT THINGS OF VALUE WITHIN THE MEANING OF THE LAW.)"

THE SECOND STATEMENT OF THIS EXCERPT IS AS FOLLOWS: "THEY'RE ILLEGAL IF THEY REQUEST MONEY OR OTHER ITEMS OF VALUE AND PROMISE A SUBSTANTIAL RETURN TO THE PARTICIPANTS."

THIS MAIL ORDER BUSINESS IS NOT A REQUEST FOR ANYTHING OF VALUE.

THIS FINANCIAL PROSPECT IS A GIFT GIVING PROSPECT.

IT CAN RIGHTLY BE CALLED U. S. MAIL NETWORKING.

READ POINT 1) OF THE ENCLOSED CIRCULAR THAT NETWORK MAILERS MAIL TO A MAILING LIST.

POINT 1): ON A PIECE OF PAPER, PRINT YOUR ADDRESS AND THIS NOTE, "ENCLOSED ARE 5 DOLLARS FOR YOU."
MAIL IT AND 5 DOLLARS TO THE ADDRESS IN POSITION 1).

AS YOU CAN SEE FROM READING THIS POINT 1) OF THE MAILING CIRCULAR, THIS IS A FINANCIAL PROSPECT NOT REQUESTING ANYTHING OF VALUE BUT RATHER IT INVOLVES GIVING TO PARTICIPANTS 5 DOLLARS.

NETWORK MAILERS WORKING THIS FINANCIAL PROSPECT ARE U. S. MAIL NETWORKERS.

IF MAILING THE ENCLOSED CIRCULAR TO A MAILING LIST INVOLVES MAILING A CHAIN LETTER, IT IS NOT AN ILLEGAL CHAIN LETTER.

AN ILLEGAL CHAIN LETTER INVOLVES REQUESTING ANYTHING OF VALUE.

MAILING THE ENCLOSED MAILING CIRCULAR IS A GIFT GIVING MAIL ORDER BUSINESS.

THIS MAIL ORDER BUSINESS IS NOT AN ENTERPRISE WHERE THERE ARE RISKS INVOLVED.
THIS MAIL ORDER BUSINESS IS NOT A CLUB WHERE NETWORK MAILERS PARTICIPATING IN THIS FINANCIAL PROSPECT MEET TO COME TO ANY AGREEMENT.
THIS MAIL ORDER BUSINESS IS AN INDEPENDENT HOME BASED BUSINESS WHERE NETWORK MAILERS MAIL OUT TO A MAILING LIST INDEPENDENTLY.

IT IS THE HUGE MARKET WHICH MAKES THIS FINANCIAL PROSPECT WORK.

MAILING $5 TO THE ADDRESS IN POSITION 1), AS INSTRUCTED IN THE MAILING CIRCULAR, DOES NOT OCCUR VERY OFTEN BECAUSE OF THIS HUGE MARKET. REPEAT POINT 1) OF THE ATTACHED MAILING CIRCULAR AS OFTEN AS YOU RECEIVE IT IN YOUR MAIL.

A GROUP OF NETWORK MAILERS REPLYING
TO NETWORK MAILERS IS WORTH PATIENTLY
WORKING FOR.
NETWORK MAILERS REPLYING TO NETWORK MAILERS
INCREASES THE RATE OF REPLY AND THE FINANCIAL
POTENTIAL.

THE MAIN IDEA IS TO CONTINUE IN THIS BUSINESS
UNTIL YOU HAVE IN YOUR RECORDS A LARGE MAILING
LIST OF NETWORK MAILERS WORKING THIS FINANCIAL
PROSPECT.

REPEAT MAILING THE ENCLOSED MAILING CIRCULAR
TO THESE REPLYING NETWORK MAILERS GREATLY
INCREASES THE RATE OF REPLY AND FINANCIAL
POTENTIAL.

WITH SUCH A LARGE MARKET, MAILING FIVE DOLLARS
TO THE ADDRESS IN POSITION 1) OF THIS MAILING
CIRCULAR DOES NOT OCCUR VERY OFTEN; HOWEVER,
YOU WILL BE RECEIVING A LARGE NUMBER OF FIVE
DOLLARS FROM THE NETWORK MAILERS WHO ARE
INVOLVED IN WORKING THIS FINANCIAL PROSPECT.

THIS WORK REQUIRES PATIENT CONTINUANCE TO ESTABLISH THIS BUSINESS.

YOUR BUSINESS IS ESTABLISHED WHEN YOU HAVE ON RECORD A LARGE NUMBER OF NETWORK MAILERS WHO ARE ALSO WORKING THIS BUSINESS.

AS THE TIME PROGRESSES, THE RATE OF NETWORK MAILERS WHO REPLY INCREASES.

IN TIME, THIS CAN AMOUNT TO $5,000,000.

HELP WHERE NEEDED MOST IS A BETTER MOTIVATION.

WHEN YOU FOCUS YOUR ATTENTION ON HELPING OTHERS, YOU HAVE PATIENCE TO CONTINUE WORKING THIS FINANCIAL PROSPECT.

TO PROCESS SUCH A LARGE AMOUNT OF INCOMING MAIL, MIGHT REQUIRE YOU TO HIRE SOME HELPERS.

$5,000,000 IS ENOUGH WORKING CASH FOR YOU TO HIRE A LOT OF HELPERS.

TO SIMPLIFY PROCESSING THIS HUGE VOLUME OF INCOMING MAIL, USE LARGE PAPER BAGS IN ORDER TO KEEP ON RECORD THE NETWORK MAILERS INVOLVED IN WORKING THIS BUSINESS.

YOU WILL BE ABLE TO PROCESS A VERY LARGE AMOUNT OF INCOMING MAIL BY THIS METHOD OF RECORD KEEPING.

MAIL TO THESE NETWORK MAILERS THE SAME CIRCULAR AS YOU FIRST MAILED.

SUMMARY

$5,000,000. MAKES THIS FINANCIAL PROSPECT WORTH WORKING TO HELP OTHERS WHERE NEEDED MOST. THE $5,000,000 IS NOT ARRIVED AT IMMEDIATELY. IT REQUIRES PATIENT CONTINUANCE IN THIS BUSINESS UNTIL YOU HAVE ON RECORD A LARGE NUMBER OF REPLYING NETWORK MAILERS.

AS A NETWORK MAILER, BE COMMITTED TO FOLLOWING THE INSTRUCTIONS OF THE ENCLOSED MAILING CIRCULAR.

THE HUGE MARKET MAKES THIS FINANCIAL PROSPECT WORK.
WHEN YOU HAVE A GROUP; FOR EXAMPLE, 1,000 NETWORK MAILERS REPLYING TO NETWORK MAILERS YOU WILL HAVE IN YOUR INCOMING MAIL A LARGE VOLUME OF WORKING CASH APPROXIMATELY EVERY TWENTY MAILING DAYS. YOUR OUTGOING GIFTS ARE VERY SMALL COMPARED TO THE INCOMING GIFTS.

THE NETWORK MAILER'S GIFT BUSINESS
FIRST, COPY THIS MAILING CIRCULAR AS IS FOR YOUR RECORD.
THIS IS AN INVITATION TO A SIGNIFICANT FINANCIAL PROSPECT.
EVERYONE WORKING THIS IS COUNTED AS A NETWORK MAILER.
HELP WHERE NEEDED MOST IS A BETTER MOTIVATION.
NETWORK MAILERS ARE COMMITTED TO FOLLOWING THESE INSTRUCTIONS.

POINTS

1). ON A PIECE OF PAPER, PRINT YOUR ADDRESS AND THIS NOTE, "ENCLOSED ARE 5 DOLLARS FOR YOU." MAIL IT AND 5 DOLLARS TO THE ADDRESS IN POSITION (1).

2). COPY THE ADDRESSES ON A PIECE OF PAPER; NOT ADDRESS (1).

3). COVER THE ADDRESSES WITH A PIECE OF PAPER 1/2 INCH WIDE.

4). REPRINT THE ADDRESSES; 2 IN 1, 3 IN 2.
PRINT YOUR ADDRESS IN POSITION (3).

5). FOR A MASTER SHEET, COPY ON 24LB, BRIGHT, WHITE COPY PAPER.

6). MAIL 100 FLYERS IN #10 ENVELOPES, PER MONTH. THIS CAN RESULT IN $5,000,000.

7). REPEAT POINT 1) AS OFTEN AS YOU RECEIVE THIS IN YOUR MAIL.

8). SECURE A COMPUTER PRINTOUT OF THIS FLYER WHENEVER NECESSARY TO KEEP CLARITY OF THE PRINT. USE BOLD FONT 12 TYPE.

9). LET REPLIERS BECOME YOUR TOP PRIORITY MAILING LIST FOR REPEATS. THIS MARKET IS VERY HUGE. IT WOULD TAKE 5 0 0 YEARS TO MAIL TO 1 50, 0 0 0, 0 0 0 DIFFERENT ADDRESSES MAILING 3 0 0, 0 0 0 YRLY.

(1). _____

(2). _____

(3). _____

IT DON'T TAKE LONG FOR ADDRESS (3) TO BE IN POSITION (1).
EVERY NETWORK MAILER HAVE THEIR TURN TO BE IN POSITION (1). AFTER (3) IS IN POSITION (1), A LOT OF 5 DOLLARS WILL FOLLOW FROM NETWORK MAILERS WORKING THIS FINANCIAL PROSPECT. NETWORK MAILERS REPLYING TO NETWORK MAILERS INCREASES THE RATE OF REPLY AND THE FINANCIAL POTENTIAL.
THE HUGE MARKET MAKES THIS FINANCIAL PROSPECT WORK.
FOR A SOURCE OF REPLY PROSPECTS, WRITE TO THE FOLLOWING FOR A FREE COPY OF THEIR ADVERTISING MAGAZINE
'SHORE TO SHORE': CHA SERVICES—P.O. BOX 1980

ROGUE RIVER, OR 97537

THE FINANCIAL POTENTIAL OF THIS BUSINESS IS WORTH THE WORKING OF IT.